A PILGRIM IN ROME

Cries of Dissent

ISBN-13: 978-0-9819000-0-1
ISBN-10: 0-9819000-0-3

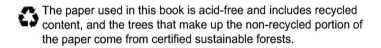 The paper used in this book is acid-free and includes recycled content, and the trees that make up the non-recycled portion of the paper come from certified sustainable forests.

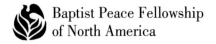 Baptist Peace Fellowship
of North America

The Baptist Peace Fellowship of North America gathers, equips and mobilizes Baptists to build a culture of peace rooted in justice. We labour with a wonderful array of peacemakers to change the world.

Al Staggs knows about words and puts them to fresh and suggestive use. He knows about brutality that shows its ugly face in too many places. And he knows about phoniness that supports evil by its default. With his words he conducts guerilla warfare, leaving us unsettled, seeing more clearly than we might wish, inviting us to decide anew. No easy slumbers here!

—Walter Brueggemann

Al Staggs writes his poetry with the passion of a prophet. Like Amos of old, he recognizes that divine worship is nothing but human justice being offered to God and that human justice is nothing but divine worship being acted out. His words call religious spokespersons and political leaders who lace their rhetoric with religious phrases alike to acknowledge both their idolatry and their hypocrisy. Read him and weep for what your country has become and for what Christianity is no more.

— John Shelby Spong

To my wife Carol, the love of my life, who so capably edited and typed this collection;

to our four children:

Ryan, Rebekah, Christa, Lisa

and our four grandchildren:

Jakob, Miah, Liana, Maya

with the fervent hope that they will one day live in a world where peace and justice prevail.

Contents

THE STATE OF THE EMPIRE

Foreword

During the past few years I have seen a number of signs and bumper stickers displaying the message *If you are not outraged, you aren't paying attention!* This statement is an accurate summary of the feelings I experience as I observe the political, religious and socio-economic climate in America today. Our nation, including much of American Christendom, has indeed succumbed to the power and influence of the military-industrial complex, which President Eisenhower so presciently warned us about upon leaving office, even as our Constitutional rights are being shredded by the government.

This collection of poetry is an attempt to give witness to my faith in the context of systemic injustice that is being proliferated on a massive scale. It is my conviction that the messages of Jesus, the prophets and the martyrs who died for speaking truth to power compel us to counter the events and evils of our time by speaking courageously on behalf of "the least of these." At some point, to be silent is to be complicit.

Al Staggs
July 6, 2007

I. Lethal
Virtues

APATHY

Death by apathy is subtle, very subtle.

Apathy never confronts its victim.

There is no contact between the apathetical one and the doomed one.

There are no sounds of pain or anguish.

Death by apathy is distant and clean.

Apathy is so impersonal as to not even take account of its victims.

Apathy vindicates itself through a maze of self-justifications and rationalizations.

Apathy reduces down to words, an inundation of verbiage and seemingly plausible platitudes.

Apathy is void of sensitivity and compassion.

Bullets kill. So does apathy.

COMPLICITY

Our citizenship in Rome
has connected us to the deplorable,
to the despicable.
All the violence perpetrated
on citizens of so many nations
and now, especially, innocent Iraqis.

We are an advanced lot,
with our sophisticated technology which
we can unleash through our impressive and
stunning array of weapons and bombs.
We are connected morally to
the actions of our young troops
whose innocence is shattered in this
immoral campaign.
The knee bone is most certainly
connected to the thigh bone
in the body of evil,
this system of greed and war.

We are the German citizens of the 30s and 40s,
where the economy ran so smoothly
in the shadow of Auschwitz
and all the other places assigned to those
who were not entitled.

We are the citizens of the South,
whose cotton industry fueled a thriving business
and dealt death and bondage
to those outside the realms
of power, wealth and influence.

We are all connected as citizens of this empire.
Our pursuits and our distractions
prevent our eyes from gazing upon
the carnage we have caused.
Yet, even in our disinterest
we are so very, very guilty
for all that is being done in the name of our nation.

Our guilt is only compounded by
our lack of concern for the other citizens
of this world – for those other sisters and brothers
in the family of God.

LEGITIMATION

No one fired a shot
or committed an evil deed.
No hateful words were spoken.
People were still
kind-spirited, generous,
taking care of their families,
civic duties, work.
They remained religious.

From kind, generous, responsible,
religious citizens
can come the most insidious evil -
the evil of silence,
of pretending to know little,
of supporting injustice
with their votes.

No right of theirs was taken,
no job of theirs was lost,
no child of theirs went hungry.
Their health care was secure.
Their taxes were covered by
exemptions, deductions,
their wealth was secured.

Sitting in their holy, hallowed
halls of worship,
hiding from the horrors
of destitution,
sustained by their
passive, sinful silence.

MUMMERY

Jesus, God, the Spirit, Bible –
words of weight
that have lost their gravity,
for they have been attached
to unjust deeds and egregious actions.

The Crusades have returned
and we Christians have become
a people of war again.

We carry our Bibles proudly
and yet are ignorant of biblical teachings.
We read texts that have lost their meaning
for our own ears,
for our own sins.

The world we are trying to save
is repulsed by our words and our message
because they are couched in xenophobic
hatred and violence.
Jesus, our friend,
has become Jesus, our fiend.

ADULTERATION

What was once previous
has become defiled, adulterated.
The Stars and Stripes
and the legacy of all those
who nobly served
and those who paid
the highest price for freedom
have been denigrated
in this nation's crusade against Iraq.

Likewise the church,
with its mission to foster peace on earth,
has become an ally
to policies of the state,
policies of death and destruction.
Churches large and small
cover the landscape of this "Christian" land.
But there is no voice
crying out from their pristine walls
against power and greed,
against our campaign of terror.

We've closed the Bible and muted its texts,
singing to God
songs with heavenly meaning
and no earthly message.
Our houses of praise afford comfort,
yet our comfort is a drug
to delude us from our duty of Dissent.
And God has nothing to say
because we, God's children, God's church,
are not listening.

The times are begging
for a message of salvation,
a message that counters
pogroms of injustice and war.
Heilsgeschicte has ceased
and we have nothing to say.

Iraqi dead testify against us,
against our vacuous professions of faith.
God, church, the Bible, our faith
have all been debased, adulterated
for national interests.

Among the clergy
there is loss of nerve,
loss of prophetic passion
in favor of church building,
increasing budgets
and carrying on business as usual.
But the message of the prophets,
the message of Jesus
whose name we claim
cries out for application
to the present moral crisis.

Silence
and comfort with the status quo
are indictments and condemnation
against the American church
which has embraced
King George as Pope.

MYOPIA

All the good people
scattered through
the little villages across this free land,
minding their concerns
and taking care of their kin.
All is well and in order
in what we see from Main Street.

But all is not well
for there are forces looming large
on the pristine prairie,
forces that reach into
the homes and pockets
of all who think
they have found security
within the walls
of a quiet little town.

SUBJUGATION

Who would ever guess
that lies could be adorned
and dressed as Truth?

Take an angry white man
from Mobile and give him a Bible
and he'll likely as not
mold the truth
to wrap around the status quo –
that the people of color and women
can go to the back of the line
in the distribution of power and privilege.

Finding the truth can come from such
simple acts of devotion
as bowing the head,
closing the eyes,
closing the hands around a Bible,
talking to an image of God in the head.

How does one hear the truth
when one is white, male and holy?
Listen to the voices of those
who are trying to get a place at the table.

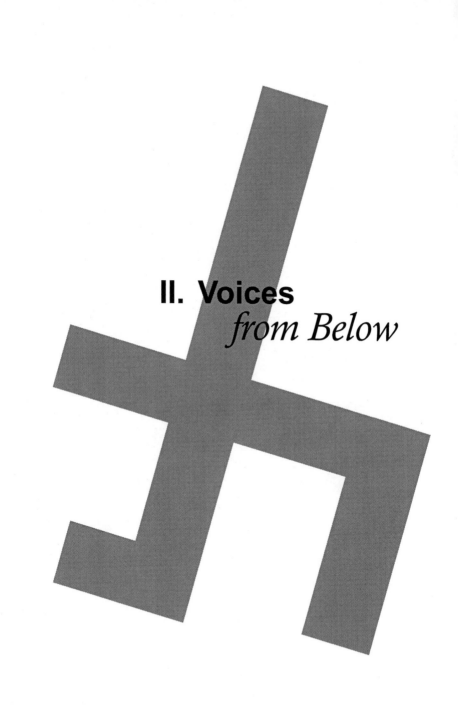

II. Voices
from Below

LISTEN TO THE VOICES
of
THE ASHES

(Upon seeing the concentration camp at Majdanek)

Listen, Listen
listen to the voices of the ashes
for they speak of redemption,
they speak of salvation.

Listen, Listen
listen to the voices of the ashes
for they speak of the conversion of
the meaning of conversion.

Listen, Listen
listen to the voices of the ashes
and learn anew about the meaning
and the place of crucifixion,
the crucifixion of the Jews.

Listen, Listen
listen to the voices of the ashes
for they tell us that those who were the
messengers of salvation are now
those who must receive salvation.
They must learn of redemption from
the voices of the ashes.

Listen, Listen
listen to the voices of the ashes.

THE CHILDREN OF LAZARUS

It's a long, long time to wait
for life to be better in that sweet by and by
for most citizens of this land
and for most of those who dwell on this earth.
For them, life is a long way
from something that is good.
It is instead something to be endured
day after agonizing day.

For those who worry about food
and housing and medical care,
life is a prison.
It is unrelenting stress to find the day's manna,
to keep something on their bellies
and to satisfy the appetites
of their young and their aged kin.

They have no time, no energy,
no freedom to organize,
to speak as one loud and compelling voice
for justice and equality.
They also have little desire to pray,
for God appears to have bequeathed
the riches and treasures of this earth
to a tiny minority,
to those who feel entitled,
those who feel deserving of their opulence.
God, they assume, is their silent partner
and so they repose
in tranquil slumber each night,
knowing that there will be quite enough
for tomorrow and many more tomorrows.

Does God know this?
Does God see this?
Does God have the power to rectify
the gap between the rich and the poor?

Surely God is not only concerned
with whether we pray
or whether we attend church on Sunday
or whether we have ever
entertained a lustful thought
or uttered words of curses.

Surely God is concerned
that there are those who sit
at the world's family table,
reach into the common platter of food
and take much more than they need,
thus depriving others around that table
of that which they need to survive.

One fact remains in this disparity –
the gulf between the haves and the have-nots
has been created, exacerbated
and perpetuated by the evils
of systemic injustice.

Those who suffer here should not
be required to wait until the hereafter
for the alleviation of their suffering.
And those who possess an abundance
should either share and work for equity
or else not look forward
to anything after this life except
that which awaits us all,
judgment.

THE VISITOR

I came to your town,
and because I was not born in your fair city
I was not included.

I came to your town
laying claim to citizenship from
what you call a "foreign" country,
so I was not included.

I came to your town,
and because I had friends of ill repute
I was not included.

I came to your town,
and because I had no material possessions
I was not included.

I came to your town,
and because I spoke with a different accent
I was not included.

I came to your town,
and because I spoke the truth
I was not included.

I came to your town
and lived and worked in the poor section
and thus was not included.

I came to your town
and you did not know me.
I am the Messiah.

SPIRITUALITY OF GRIEF

The pall of grief
has found a home in my spirit of late.
It has become my spirituality.
Sorrow has become a daily thing
that cannot be assuaged or find relief.
I grieve for my nation,
whose policies have become evil.
I grieve over its leader,
whose unjust decisions have brought
discredit to his office
and to our standing in the world.

I grieve for my flag,
symbol of the liberty and justice which
millions have purchased at the highest cost.
The Stars and Stripes has been tarnished
and made to mean something
that is foreign to its ideal.

I grieve for young men and women
who have been commissioned to carry out
the orders of a Commander-in-Chief
who has lost his way, lost his soul.
I see the pictures of youth
who have given their lives and their futures
for a cause that has only brought
death and destruction to the world
and I grieve.

I grieve for Iraqis who have endured
the violation of their sovereignty
and suffered incalculable losses of
life, property and dignity.

I read accounts of the deaths of thousands
of Iraqi women, children and men
at the hands of our forces
and this news plunges me deeper into
ever greater grief and rage.
These deaths are not counted by our government
because they do not count.

We have become what we most feared.
By unleashing this endless cycle of violence,
we have become the terrorists.

I grieve for those who know and yet are silent.
Their silence condemns them and us
and gives assent to those who wage this war.

We know nothing of God.
We know nothing of Jesus, the Prince of Peace.
We have become demons of death.

I grieve for my faith,
for the words of scripture that
have been omitted from our Sunday sermons
and left to remain mute in the crisis we face.

I grieve for the One whose Name I profess
and cannot understand those who also
profess that Name and yet support
our campaign of deadly terror.
Yet they do, enthusiastically, openly,
while indoctrinating their large flocks
on the "merits" of our nation's hellish work.
Grieving at this misuse of my faith,
I also rage.

If all I knew of Jesus
was what these "national prophets" profess,
I could never be a Christian.

Grieving has become my spirituality.
In the spirit of the prophets
who grieved over their people,
in the spirit of Jesus
who grieved over Jerusalem,
I grieve for my people
and the people of Iraq
and the ideals we have smeared
in our contract with evil.

MARVIN GAYE, WHERE ARE YOU?

Marvin, how we miss your soulful voice
and the courage you had to ask "What's goin' on?"
You were a prophet in song
in the midst of that awful war,
terrible times of death and destruction
when so many of us found solace in our silence.

Now we need you again.
We need you to again ask that question,
"What's goin' on?"
For we've become accustomed to insanity.
We've lost our moral compass.
We've become an evil empire
that is wrecking havoc on the earth.

Let us play your song again and again
to shake us from our lethargy, our apathy,
to ask what we are doing in the name of God.
Let us hear your plaintive cry today.
Marvin, Marvin, how we miss your voice.

FEELING LIKE A BLACK MAN

The melodies, the lyrics,
the major keys of white kids
singing songs of faith
do not touch me like
the earthy, groaning protests of anguish
set to music by black people
who sing their songs from memory,
a memory laced with their desperation
in the search for truth amid horror.

The contexts of our lives
dictate the tonalities of our songs.
The settings of our lives
dictate the lyrics we join to our tunes.
For it's not just heaven that is at stake.
It is singing in the midst of hell,
it is proclaiming the timeless truth
in a world of countless trials –
this is music, this is worship, this is soul.

SHOUT IT AGAIN, LORD

Godly sort of folks, I see
running out in front of the political march,
waving banners for moral values,
carrying their half-read Bibles.
Godly, conservative, white-faced folks,
throwbacks to slave owners using the Word
to justify their deeds,
to numb their hearts.

Remember this!
Remember this!
Remember this!
No one –
not the curser,
not the drug addict,
not the drunkard,
not the prostitute,
not the murderer,
not the prayerless pagan –
no one,
no one
is as immune to the substance of the Word
as those who embrace that Word
and then live
lives of compassionless compromise –
those who preach a relative gospel,
those who espouse power
and never question,
those for whom wealth is a right
and poverty inconceivable.

Their Savior, their Lord preached
to his own hometown that he came
to bring good news to the poor,
to liberate the oppressed,
and he was nearly murdered.

That Savior should come again and
shout the message today, this year,
this next political year.
Shout the good news
to give hope to the poor,
the elderly,
the children,
the disenfranchised,
the immigrant,
the farm worker,
the disabled.

Shout the liberating good news
that change, that conversion
must come not only to hearts.
Change must come to the practices of
white-faced heirs of slave owners
who are trying to bring
slaves back to the plantations,
who are trying to widen the gap between
those who get what they want
and those who do without.

Shout it again, Lord.
Shout it again, Lord.
Shout it for our time!

REFLECTIONS ON AN EMPTY TOMB

The Easters pass
and the stories of empty tombs
and a risen savior are told with fervor
from a million pulpits,
but the tragedy of the Cross remains.
God's creation travails under the
strain of her humanity.
For if Jesus is found among
the beggars, the prisoners, the orphaned,
the hungry, the homeless, the abused,
the penniless, the overworked,
then Christ still suffers on the Cross.
There can be no complete Resurrection
until we are all resurrected,
until we are all liberated.

How cheaply we celebrate the Easter story
with each passing year
while mouths go unfed,
while abusers keep tormenting their victims.
How dare we experience the ecstasy
of our sublime liturgies
while hell continues to rain
on God's helpless children.

What in Hell is going on?
What in Heaven is going on?
History is still unfolding and still ringing in our ears.
I wait, I hope, I hurt and I hope.

PROPHECY

And where will all of this end?
Where will all of the unbridled greed
and the lust for warring
take this, our powerful Empire?

There are ominous signs on our horizon
to indicate that our stability
might soon be tested and tried.

How long can the richest continue
to get richer on the backs of the
tens of millions who labor for little,
those who cannot afford gas, nor the car,
those who struggle to pay the rent
and to find a place in their measly budgets
for medical bills and prescriptions?

How long will it be before those millions
tire of paying the tax bill while
their vital services are cut to the bone
and defense contractors and oil companies
bathe themselves in their massive fortunes?

How long will it be before those millions
take to the street and bring
this affluent society to a standstill?

How long will it take for the poor to realize that
though they have not the wealth of this nation,
they nevertheless can collectively
dislodge the status quo?

And when will the religion of this land
serve the interests of the poor and oppressed
in a manner that is reminiscent of the Exodus,
where the children of Israel found liberation
from the injustice and oppression
of Egypt and Pharaoh?

When will the representatives of religion discover
their prophetic voice and rail against
a State that is dealing death to its poorest citizens
by sending their children to war
while increasing the coffers of its wealthiest citizens?

Perhaps the State's chaplains cannot take
the risk of speaking since they also receive
the same generous tax breaks as the wealthy.

The church has become a gated community
of style with no substance.
The issues of injustice and war cannot
penetrate the walls of these monuments,
these idols of pride,
nor can they find a place in the weekly sermons
of those who profess to speak for God.

The Scriptures have become irrelevant.
Jesus has become little more than a symbol.
The application of biblical truths
has been watered down,
reduced to matters merely of the heart.

The suffering of the poor in this our land of Empire
is nothing short of the continuation
of the crucifixion of Jesus,
for He is them and they are Him.

And those of us who build our wealth
through unjust systems, with no thought
of the consequences to the poor,
are the perpetrators.

Where will all the glaring inequality take us?
The rich will likely not change the
systems that so lavishly reward them.
Change will likely only occur,
radically and suddenly,
when the poor and disenfranchised
understand that God never willed this to be,
that God is with them in their struggle
for justice, for liberation, for a New Land.

WHITE FOLKS FROM PODUNK

Good, nice, righteous white men from Podunk,
they see their demise in all of their lies
as they hear the voices of the red man, the soul man
and their own lovely wives.

Lord save us from the white folks from Podunk.
Save us from the people who've stolen your word
and shackled the bodies and souls
of millions of poor and powerless foes.

They all seemed to be believing, dedicated souls
who carried their Bibles close to their sides
but had never really looked inside.

Oh Jesus, come down and see the
kind of folk who've stolen your name, who've
stolen your cross and brought you such shame.

Lord save us from the good folks from Podunk,
those people who bless us to go to their wars.
They are heirs to the keepers of the Third Reich.
Lord save us from them, show us the door.

YELLING FOR JUSTICE

Those who claim
to speak for Christ these days
espouse views that are offensive,
immoral, unjust, just plain insane.

Those of us who disagree
with these voices of distortion
are forced to the sidelines,
advised to pretend that we agree
since we also call ourselves "Christians."

Not so. Our very souls are defiled by these
greedy mouthpieces of conservative causes,
these nationalists,
these fascists disguised as fighters for freedom.
Christ is not a part of this.
Cannot be.

And so we, those of us who disagree with the
dominant "Christian" culture,
are forced to yell louder and to speak in ways
that shock even our own sensibilities.
It is the only possible way to counter this
propaganda that passes for truth.

We must yell and we must offend
in order to be heard at all.

A WOMAN'S PLACE

Where, oh where did we men get
all these loony notions and oppressive views
that women are inferior, unequal to men?

This view is especially ugly
in the life of a church.
In far too many churches we have
consigned woman to her "rightful"
God-ordained place
as second-class citizen with nothing to say.

This is entitlement at its worst,
the worst form of abuse,
for it is carried out in the name of God
with Bible in hand.

How long will it take us, we men,
to come to terms with our cultural captivity
and the fact that we do not read
the scriptures through eyes of comprehension
but through the prism of our own prejudice?

Ask black people,
ask the Jews
to understand the favored status
we have bestowed upon ourselves
as Caucasian males.

We owe our women of faith far, far more than this.
Mary, the mother of Jesus,
Anna the prophetess,
Deborah, Rebekah
to name a few.

We owe the matriarchs of our clans,
our grandmothers and mothers,
whose faith, sacrifice and nurturing
shaped our lives.
What a debt we owe them.

Let us repent of our arrogance,
our mistaken sense of privilege,
and ordain proudly, publicly, thankfully
all those who live
their womanly lives among us.

Our very existence and our knowledge of faith
are directly attributable to
their fore-ordained places of ministry
in the lives of all men everywhere.

CAMPESINO

Body of burden, toiling endless hours
'neath a merciless sun
with eyes bound to the hard, hot earth.

I wish for you, o campesino,
to raise your eyes to the silent,
transcendent skies, to perhaps hope
as you have never hoped.

God did not will your plight,
as he did not will my life of ease.

Campesino, we are brothers bound together,
for you are a judgment on me.
You are a judgment on us all.

SEMINARY 1954

White, white-faced boys of theology
dressed in starched white shirts
and pin-striped suits
of gray, blue and black,
folding hands to pray and
discussing how to save the lost.

Black, yellow, brown and women
are not here.
They are out there,
outside the classroom
and the seminary,
outside this exclusive club, a ghetto
of a fast-vanishing theology.

Black, Yellow, Brown, Women –
holding the keys to salvation
for white-faced boys of theology.

III. The Adulteration
of Religion

THE CROSS

The Cross
Simple
Crude
Ugly
Ghastly
Applied to common criminals; a punishment of humiliation, of excruciating agony, of death; a tragic symbol of the crime of all time, the crucifixion of the Son of God; epitome of banishment, relegated to its place outside the gates.

The Cross,
atop stately
structures
of advanced
civilizations.
Now within
the city gates.
Worn by the
inhabitants
in gold, in
silver, with
diamonds.
Adorning
magnificent
edifices,
established
in society's
mainstream.
Massive
Shining
Artistic
Esthetic
Accepted
Co-opted

THE MANGER

Sweet little Jesus Child
born in that manger
on a cold, dark night
in a stable,
an outbuilding for animals.

The King of Kings,
the Prince of Peace
surprised the world.
He was not born into
the king's court in a big city.
He was not born into riches,
but poverty.
No one had any room
for his Mama and Daddy,
no place for him to stay.

What if he were born today?
Where would he be born?
Would it be New York,
or London, or LA, maybe Rome,
or maybe Paris, do you think?
Who would his parents be?
Doctors, lawyers,
statesmen, do you think?

No. If he were born today,
he would be born to lowly
campesinos in Nicaragua.
He would be born to refugees
in El Salvador, fleeing from the
threat of the death squads who
would have surely sought him out.

He would be born to Ethiopians
trudging their way along
a desert floor searching
for food and shelter from the cold.

He would be born in the ghettos
of Johannesburg, or Calcutta,
or Sao Paulo, or Juarez, or Detroit.
His parents would be among those
whose meager benefits had been
cut by compassionless politicians.

And would we notice him today?
No. Not at all.

So why do we pay homage
to the manger scene?
We place it in our lovely homes,
on our manicured lawns,
in our beautiful churches,
in the center of our thriving towns,
all the while neutralizing its
thunderous meaning.
We make friends with the baby Jesus,
robbing him of his hostility
to our selfish and secure ways.

THE RELIGION SHOW

We can keep "In God We Trust" on our coins,
retain "one nation under God" in our pledge,
place the Ten Commandments
on every courthouse lawn,
pray during every class in our schools
and go to church every Sunday
to pray for our troops and
pledge allegiance to our nation's flag,
which stands proudly and conspicuously
in the center of our halls of worship –
but none of that changes the fact
that we, as a nation, are waging monstrous terror.

The president said God told him to bomb Iraq,
but it wasn't God the Iraqis saw
in our impressive campaign of "shock and awe."
It isn't God the poor of the world see
as we wage war to control other nations' oilfields
and line the pockets of corporate executives
and stockholders.

We can profess Jesus as our Savior unceasingly,
but profession without practice is empty.
Piosity without peacemaking is meaningless.
Promoting family values without
pursuing justice for all is hypocrisy.
They are all just words, hollow words,
orthodoxy without orthopraxis.
The greatest evils are those which are
committed in the name of God,
and those who advocate unjust war and
find security in their "profession" of faith in God
suffer from the most acute delusions.

We go to war and victimize thousands
and say "Lord, Lord."
We send our poorest children to combat
and say "Lord, Lord."
We demonize Islam and other religions
and say "Lord, Lord."
We build our massive temples of worship
and say "Lord, Lord."
Yet our understanding of God's word
is as empty as those temples
on a Monday morning.

We may have to wait until the judgment
to hear the Lord answer
"Get away from me, you religious charlatans.
I never knew you."

CAESAR EST KURIOS

In this season of remembrance of Jesus
who was born in Nazareth,
sons and daughters of Rome
are being sacrificed to Caesar,
giving their lives and futures
for the purposes of the empire
and laying waste a land and a people
already ravaged by poverty.

And all the while the citizens of Rome
are participating in their annual orgy –
their liturgy of lights
and their offering of lavish gifts
to bolster the economy of the empire.

A graven, obscene service of sacrifice it is,
co-opting the meaning of the message
of this Jesus, this Prince of Peace,
to increase the wealth and power of the empire
on the backs of those who have no place
in the inn, who are themselves
running from Caesar.

The citizens of Rome are
impressive in their demonstration
of homage to this Jesus,
but the place of highest devotion
has been supplanted by Caesar.
So this year, in this our land of the empire,
our gifts, our children and our allegiance to Jesus
are being given instead to the state
where Caesar, not Jesus, is lord.

BLINDED BY SIGHT

And God came to us
in our own time,
but we could not behold his image
for our eyes were blinded
by the culture that had taught
and convinced us
that we are the chosen people.

We could not hear God's message
because it came wrapped
in black, red, brown
and yellow skin
and spoke in a different accent
from our own familiar one.

We were deaf to truth,
those of us who suffered
from the great delusion
that we are the only true bearers of
God's word and knowledge.

We never understood
that God was speaking to us
and not through us.

LET'S CALL OFF CHURCH THIS SUNDAY

Let's call off church this Sunday.
Let us not gather to pray and sing.
May we not speak this Sunday
of the sacred texts of our choosing
and the familiar interpretations
we assign them.

May we instead take this day
to ponder the plight of those
whose lives Jesus came to save,
the poor and oppressed
in our land and the world over.

Let us not cloud the issues
of systemic violence and war
that we have fostered
through our silence,
through our acceptance
of systems of destruction.
This silence and acceptance have
made our professions of faith
sound empty and hollow
to a world that needs more
than words, prayers and hymns.

Let us not sit in the places
of our holy comfort and
delude ourselves through
banal rituals of religiosity
that we are not conspirators
of injustice and war against
the sick, the hungry, the oppressed,
against Jesus himself.

May we reflect this day
upon the meaning of the Cross
to those who are crucified every day
because we ignore and thereby
condone the havoc wreaked
by our instruments of death.

May we cease this one day
from the familiarity of our meetings
and the delusions they breed.
Let us not speak this day
of salvation and redemption,
for salvation and redemption
cry out for expression
in the laws and deeds
of this our nation, Babylon.

COMPARATIVE RELIGION

It is believed
among many Christian circles
that all Muslims are bent on terror.
Yet I hear the sounds of terror
in the voices of Robertson,
Falwell and their kind.

Reminds one of the KKK,
who spouted scripture
as they terrorized African-Americans.
Reminds one of the Reich church
who saluted the Fuehrer
as they ignored the plight of Jews.
Reminds one of the religious folk
who upheld apartheid
as they said their prayers.

And now we are destroying Iraq,
we good, Bible-believing, moral people.
Iraqi children have been
buried by the thousands
and we don't feel remorse.

So whose God is the one true God –
Allah or the God who we believe
sanctions *our* brand of terror?

ELEPHANT IN THE ROOM

There's no need to talk about it,
no need to bring it up.
Not this Sunday.
Not any Sunday.
The lectionary did not proscribe it
so we won't mention it
this Sunday
or any Sunday.

Controversy could ensue –
phone calls, emails, letters
storming the pastor's desk.
People would harangue
so it's not worth it.
Building programs await,
committees to meet with,
visitors to see,
lectures to write,
sermons to prepare,
phone calls to make.

Keep everybody happy.
Don't make a wave
by bringing up
the elephant in the room,
that our nation is murdering Iraqis
and subjecting our soldiers
to death and dismemberment.

Let's all agree not to talk about it
and it just won't be there.
Yet our silence
cannot hide the facts.
They will not go away.

Perfunctory and innocuous
prayers at every service,
praying for the president
and our leaders.
These prayers are not working
for there is no light in this government,
nothing but war, war, war
and oil and greed and weapons.

And all the president's euphemisms
of liberty, terror, freedom,
sanctity of human life
cannot hide the truth
of what he is doing –
killing and torturing
an already oppressed people.

I wonder where Jesus is.
Residing in our polished,
pristine temples?

Our services of worship
are drama, theater.
We ignore the elephant
and rehearse our piety
while blood flows in Iraq.
What a paradox.
What a blasphemy.
All our talk about values
and morality is farce.
If we cannot speak
about the elephant,
we have nothing
meaningful to say.
Nothing at all.

PIOUS PARADOX

"The stained glass is certainly
lovely. So are the padded
pews in their 'rich' color."

The smell of death is
pervasive. The sight of
dying, in its various
stages, is all around.

"We've been praying for
this new sanctuary. It will
be a testimony to the
community. What a glorious
work of architecture!"

The children have
bloated bellies. Hundreds
of little children too sick to
cry. What hope is there for
them?

"The choir will be wearing
new robes – 100 strong,
beautiful voices ringing the
rafters with praise."

They can't cry or even
whimper. The parents do,
though. Big questions
with no answers.

"Certainly we'll be able to
pay for this. God will provide
for us. How blessed we are.
How blessed we have been.
How blessed we will be!"

No land for tilling. No
power, no luck. There is
only today, possibly.

"Let's have a banquet next
month and honor all of our
leading deacons. What a
great tribute it will be."

Two deaths occur.
One in Africa, the death of a people.
The other in America, the death of a conscience.
And the latter is the greatest tragedy of all.

THE PASSION OF THE CHRIST

Wearying are all of the
depictions of the
suffering of our Lord,
whose dying and death
are "performed" in so many
passion plays and cantatas
and now in another
epic motion picture.

All of this is so tiring to my
senses and sensibilities.
These performances miss
the point, which is that
Jesus is being oppressed,
tortured and murdered
every single day in
the lives of millions upon
millions of the naked,
the sick, the hungry and
the thirsty of our world.

Did he not tell us ever so plainly
that he was embodied in all of
those who suffer in our time?

While the Church has performed
its ritual of remembrance
of the "passion of Christ"
throughout her history,
innumerable souls have
tasted very real torture
and very real death.

Have we in the Church
been more concerned,
perhaps, with our
dramatic performances
than with the plight of
those whom Jesus
said he was to be?

Oberammergau's passion
play continued to flourish
during the Nazi regime,
when Jews were being
dragged away by the
millions to death camps.

Let us weep for Jesus, yes,
but let us also weep for
those who are being
crucified this very day.

BASE ECONOMICS

A lot of talk about God these days
on the television and from groups
who want to put prayer in the schoolhouse
and the commandments in the courthouse.
So much loud talk coming from these
well-dressed "profits" in the glamour of
their well-endowed sanctuaries
and greatly subsidized ministries.

I hear what you say, "profits," and yet
I can't seem to take my eyes off
the accoutrements of your success
that do so impress me.
My, how God has blessed you!

It's good of you, dear "profits,"
to stand up for all that is right and true
and to help us know that our once
Christian nation is being destroyed
by the promiscuity of all the sexual
marketing of Hollywood and the
morality of our former president.
And we do know and do feel the
current of our culture's infatuation
with all that is not pure.

Oh, but there is another kind of lust that
has taken hold, not only of our nation's soul.
It has also snared those who pose as
proclaimers of God's truth, yet the Truth
has escaped these impressive, well-dressed,
well-heeled manipulators of the pocketbooks
and the minds of poor vulnerable souls.

Put down those Bibles, "profits,"
for you do not know what it
says to our day and our time.
Robbery and greed are
killing the spirit of God's children.
The devil of greed has taken
the soul of this nation hostage
and not only are you, dear "profits,"
not exempt – you are leading
the devil's charge.

Why don't you talk about this
insidious cancer of avarice from your
lofty, well-endowed pulpits of power?
It's not prudent, is it, "profits?"

So you can yell all you want about
the lewdness of this sick society
and you can raise your hands and
praise your idolatrous image of God,
but it is all just empty chatter
with absolutely no biblical basis.
You are nothing but parodies of truth,
and if all we knew about Jesus was
what we see in the manipulative
affectations of your garish shows,
some of us could never believe in
a so-called savior who was born
in a lowly stable to parents of poverty.

You wealthy, overfed "profits" of
a false messiah: it is you, most of all,
who need to be reached by the
very word you speak to us.

GLORY, GLORY HALLELUJAH

Glory, glory hallelujah,
God's truth is marching on.
But what manner of God is this that we espouse?
A god who declares preemptive war, murdering
and maiming over 100,000 innocent Iraqis
on the basis of propaganda and fear-mongering?
A god who sacrifices America's best
at the altar of our nation's avarice?

This is the god of the religious wrong,
the self-appointed prophets who speak ex-cathedra,
the arrogant and biblically ignorant opportunists
who commit blasphemy from their wealthy pulpits,
the blind guides who lead their blind sheep
to believe that all will be well if they pray
and support "God's man."
I've seen the man and he has no marks of godliness,
only marks of hate, lies, arrogance and hubris.
There is no compassion in his eyes,
no grief over the body count of ours or theirs.
There is no thought of the plight of the poor,
only thoughts of how to further enrich the rich.
This is not God's man.
This is a monster of our own making.

These blind guides are legion in our land,
but their voices are not the voices of God's word.
Theirs are voices that accommodate the mighty,
the rich and the powerful of our nation.
These manipulators play on the fears
of ordinary citizens and dictate to their followers
what they are to believe, how they are to vote,
who they are to hate.

We have fashioned a god in our own image
based upon our fears
and our all-encompassing need for security.
But all of our fire power and technology of destruc-
tion
will not save us.
They will only further condemn us in the
eyes of the one true God
who has a preferential option for the oppressed,
the poor, the victims.
And we are none of those.

The one true God has chosen to be silent and
allow us to reap the wages of our ways.

ICE A JESUS

Eisegesis and *Exegesis*:

Ice a Jesus is a cold reading of the texts
and it's a good one to have
if you are the Klan or the Nazis or Us.
Finding an appropriate text is needful
to fashion our xenophobia
and make us righteous soldiers of good
against all that we deem evil.

Take a text and the teachings of Jesus
and mold them to your whims.
It helps to have a church
with willing crowds to hear.
Add hymns and prayers
and Ice a Jesus can sound just right.

Ice a Jesus has served many a good cause –
slavery, racism, apartheid, fascism, sexism,
anti-Semitism and nationalism
just to name a few.
Great causes require moral authority.

Ex a Jesus requires painstaking skill,
sensitivity to the Spirit
and the possibility of reform.
These would never further our cause,
so Ice a Jesus will serve us just fine.

RECRUCIFIED

Jesus died among his own,
murdered amid his countrymen.

And he dies again among
those who claim to be his kin.

They have put him to death
a second time while giving
utterance to his words.

Praises, sermons, prayers
form a cacophony of farce
as though they were lauding him
beneath a cross of their making.

And they tell the world
of the "truth" of the savior
they never knew.

FAMILY VALUES

We are seeing a resurgence.
The Crusades are upon us –
Christians "witnessing" by demonizing others,
seeking to wrest control of the government,
preaching an accommodated "truth"
that is tailor-made for
aspiring young professionals
eager to find their places of
power at the table.

Oh, these are well-dressed men and women
with the scent of success
and no shortage of cash,
no lack of confidence or hubris.
Oh, these are the people who
make noise about "family values."

Family values, huh?
Think about Mary and Joseph
trying to find a place to start in the land
where being poor and transient
means certain robbery,
not by the criminals in the street
but by squeaky-clean "good" people
who have made greed a family value
and injustice the price of success.

TALKIN' 'BOUT JESUS

My goodness, there's lots of folks
talkin' 'bout Jesus – what would Jesus do,
what he said in the Good Book.
But there's not much talkin'
'bout what Jesus would say
or what he would do when it comes
to the burning issues of our day.
Naw, that's too much of a risk.
Folks might get offended.
After all, one has to respect folks'
political sensibilities.
So we keep on repeatin'
the familiar, the safe words,
the ones that don't challenge
our views, our ways, our politics.

Churches are meetin' and praisin' Jesus,
reverin' his holy name
while we're sendin' our kids
to fight the government's demonic war.
We call it "fightin' for our freedoms"
and we don't give it a thought
that we're robbin' thousands
of God's children of their freedoms
by puttin' them in early graves.

We're keepin' our flags posted
front and center in our churches
so we can remember our allegiance,
the one that seems to equal
our allegiance to Jesus
with our flags so prominent there.

The preachers talkin' 'bout Jesus these days
don't mention war, social injustice,
poverty or the environment.
That's just not wise, not prudent.
It's too controversial, too uncomfortable
to be spoutin' off 'bout what Jesus
would do or say about those issues.
So they talk instead 'bout family values
and other folks' personal morality.

No one's *really* talkin' 'bout Jesus.

CHRISTMAS 2006

Sparkling lights everywhere,
manger scenes on the lawns of churches and
houses,
Christmas is here again.
But the lights cannot alter the darkness in our land.
The message of the Prince of Peace has been lost.
It has been rejected in favor of the national policies
of war, of torture, of greed, of stealing from the poor.

And we beheld His glory,
the image of an Iraqi baby born in lowly Baghdad.
We bring him gifts of white phosphorous,
rockets, machine guns and grenades.

The Advent season observances have little to do
with meaning and much to do with form and custom.
His birth has been commercialized, trivialized.
It is irrelevant to our time.
We can only see Jesus from afar, 2000 years ago.
Let us leave Him there to salve our conscience,
to happily delude ourselves that we are the children
of the One who came to bring Peace on Earth.

How can we dare honor the child
who came to liberate the oppressed when,
by our policies, our votes, our lifestyles,
we give evidence that we are the oppressors.

That poor little child, that refugee
born under the specter of Roman domination
has little in common with us, the dominators.
The manger scene doesn't fit, it's out of place.
It should be to us an offense,
an indictment of all that we have become.

We cannot sing loud enough
to drown out the cries from Mosul, from Fallujah,
from Abu-Ghraib, from Guantanamo
and from the homes of grief-stricken families
who have lost their loved ones on the fields
of battles that should have never been waged.
We don't need the spirit of drink in this season
for we have already become intoxicated
on our power and our military might.

And it is in this season that we offer our billions
to confirm where our real trust lies –
not in God, but in our arms.
We've given the arms dealers a blank check
and offered pocket change for the needy.

There's no room this Christmas
for the likes of Jesus and his family,
not in our budgets nor in our hearts.
We'll collect our baskets of food for the poor
but that won't make a dent in the needs of those
who have been robbed by our policies
and our systems of greed that reward
more to those who already "have"
and less to those who have next to nothing.

We might as well just sing nursery rhymes
this Christmas rather than pretend that we
honor the Christ child with the old familiar carols.
They cannot be heard above the wailing
of all those who are victims of our national hate
and our national greed.
So this Christmas I will remember the Christ child
and I will grieve.

CONVERSION TO ATHEISM

Injustice has become a way of life.
We can no longer feel,
no longer think about the crimes
committed by those who possess power.

We are numbed in the myopia
of our everyday concerns,
living in denial of all
that is being perpetrated on us
and on the Iraqi people.

Where is the outcry?
Where is the protest?
The media has joined hands
with this fascism falsely cloaked
in the garments of democracy.
And those who claim to speak for God
have blasphemed the Almighty
before their vast television audiences.

If it is God who is directing
the policies of this corrupt and
ruthless administration, as so many
evangelical leaders have claimed,
consider me an atheist.

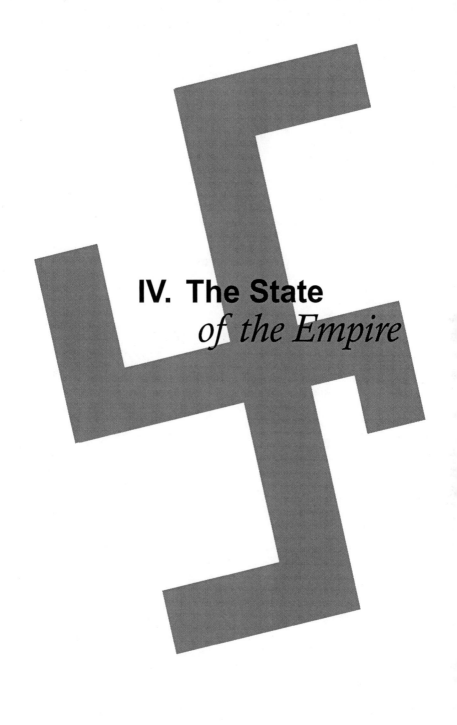

IV. The State
of the Empire

NATIONAL SECURITY

Sleek steeled
symbols of security
point to the skies,
erect, silent,
rusting as they wait
for the enemy
of American interests.

The enemy
has already struck.
The adversary
attacked our cities,
leaving them
defenseless, hopeless.
The next target
was the economy,
gutted and pillaged
by this ravenous force.
The enemy then
stole food and medicine
from the poor
of our land.
Next, the conquering
forces occupied
the halls of education.

Those sleek steeled
symbols of security
are the enemies,
standing there
erect, impotent,
yet warring against
our national interests.

A TRAIN GOING THE WRONG WAY

"If you board the wrong train, it is no use running along the corridor in the other direction."   —Dietrich Bonhoeffer

Like a train going the wrong way
is our war on Iraq.
We Americans are all passengers
on this murderous and maddening journey.
Nothing we could say can change
the truth about our ghastly folly.
And there is nothing we can do
to change the fact that we are invaders
who are pillaging a land of its resources
and bringing immeasurable suffering
to the citizens of that nation,
who do not want us there.

We are passengers on this train bound for hell.
Yet we delude ourselves into believing
that we are combating terrorism,
that we are removing WMDs,
that we are spreading freedom and democracy,
that we, as Americans, are invincible to defeat,
that we will not be judged by history,
that God is on our side,
that if we can just pour enough
money and munitions into the effort
and send enough of our bravest and finest,
we are certain to win, to prevail.

This is the delusion of a passenger
who rises from his seat and walks
in a direction opposite from that of the train –
that this gesture will make everything right.

The train began its awful journey
in March of 2003
and there is nothing we can do or say
to change or make right what we have done
and what we are continuing to do to Iraq
while squandering our precious resources
that could have been used beneficially
to bring justice and equality
to the citizens of our own land.

And we all bear responsibility for dealing Death
to those who continue to give their lives
for this spurious cause,
as well as to those who continue to experience
the horrific effects of our military might.

We are all passengers on the Train to Hell.

BLESSED ARE THE WARMAKERS

Blessed are the war makers
for they shall be called
the sons and daughters of Satan,
and so we are.

We've dishonored the Savior's
name and his purpose
with the madness of our
militant methods.

Our leaders have perverted
the message of the old hymn,
"Onward Christian soldiers
marching as to war
with the cross of Jesus
going on before."

The missionaries will follow,
telling the poor misguided Muslims
the story of Jesus.
We'll give them the word on the
heels of our murderous rampage.

The office of Fatherland Security
has declared an Orange Alert
for Bush is on the loose.

Fighting terrorism?
We only exacerbate that problem as we,
the land of the free and the brave,
continue to carry out gutless acts of horror
upon nations both far and near.

Ask, if you could, the graves
in El Salvador and Nicaragua.
Ask Archbishop Romero, who
was martyred through the intrigues
of our Graduate School of Terror,
nestled in the sleepy,
tranquil village of Columbus.

Americans, stricken with
gullibility and naiveté,
continue to embrace
the half-truths fed to them
by the spin and sound bites
of our caricature of kingship.

Baghdad fell
and so did we.
They lost their war.
We lost our soul.

Such bravery, such valor.
Our 400 billion dollar force
was ordered to squash a
fledgling army that could muster
only one billion for its cause.
Such heroism, such courage.
Such cowardice.

Our children will play with toy guns
and tanks, shooting the bad guys,
then they'll go to Sunday School
to learn about Jesus,
who did not carry a weapon.
Raise our schizophrenic offspring well.
Train them in the ways of war
and be sure to give them Jesus.

THE NEXT REICH?

Like civilizations past,
we suffered from our delusion
that we were the chosen,
that we were the last word as regards Truth.
Our wealth and our strength
only confirmed the rightness of our cause.
And body bags are flown to a faraway place
to bring our children and grandchildren home
after our cause and our enemies are executed.
And the bodies of women, children and old men
lay scattered on the landscape of a foreign land.
But we will have no camera to record
the results of our wanton murder,
so few back home will know.
Few will be troubled.

We will continue to live our lives as before,
drinking deep from the wells of the world's oil
to satisfy our insatiable and expensive tastes.
And we will go to our churches on Sunday
and sing "God Bless America."
But can God hear our blasphemous chorus
when the armies of our nation commit murder
under the orders of the emperor
who, the world knows, is wearing no clothes?

And silence has taken hold of the tongues
of this nation's so-called "prophets"
for they are afraid to offend those
who supply their gold.
They are afraid not to hold high the flag,
our flag which, for much of the world,
resembles a twisted cross.

SECRETARY OF OFFENSE

Our Secretary of Offense
outranks the privates, the sergeants
and every general.
He even outranks Goebbels
'cause Goebbels is dead,
yet our secretary suffers
from the same character flaw.

This bespectacled civilian
takes pride in his vicarious victory.
Winning wars is a heady thing.
Its addiction can only be cured by defeat,
but shock and awe are working for now
so let's keep the celebration going
with more of this drug.

He has identified the "axis of evil"
and summoned the "allies,"
or should I say the "coalition" of two
to erase the dangers of terror.
And the coalition of two waged
their noble war
against the suspected foes.
Yet the foes are increasing in every nation,
for they are not armies.
They are desperate people everywhere
who take offense at our national "defense."

THE STATE OF THE UNION

The flow of oil is lessening,
but the blood continues to flow unabated.
Iraq, the great war,
has now become a debacle
and all we can do is wag our heads
and distract ourselves
with our petty entertainments
and listen to the news which is not news.
We don't know where we're headed,
nor do we seem to care.

This nation,
this great nation of Washington and Lincoln,
is being guided by neo-cons
who, with each new directive,
increasingly resemble fascists.
But we do not care, for our
little lives have not been disturbed,
yet.

It will happen when enough citizens
have had enough of the gross inequity
between the rich and the poor,
when increasing numbers of Americans
cannot afford to purchase health insurance,
when more and more hard-working people
cannot make ends meet,
when more and more of our youth
pay with limb and with life.
When an increasing number of our children
go to bed and go to school hungry
for a war that was waged on falsehoods,
there will inevitably be unrest.

In the face of this war
and the rapidly growing disparity
between our rich and our poor,
our religiosity appears to be a sham.
The pulpits of our churches
have nothing to say about the real issues.
The rituals continue unchanged, and so do we.
Our worship has become blasphemous,
all our praise seems meaningless
in the face of the destruction
we have caused to God's special children –
those who are poor, the oppressed,
the victims of this world.

We "moral" people have not the capacity
to feel sorrow and horror at what we see
and hear about our campaigns of terror.
It is our nation, after all,
and our nation is always right.

So much violence cannot be inflicted
without a price to be paid by us,
our children and our grandchildren.
For now there is the illusion of stability,
but it cannot last.
The war that we have maliciously waged
will most certainly engulf our economy,
our way of life, our security,
our peace of mind.

The highest measure of our morality
may be to resist the forces who expect
obedience in the name of patriotism,
to say "no" to those who would have us
kneel before the altar of the state
and defile our very souls.

OPERATION IRAQI FREEDOM

Iraq has been capitalized, not democratized.
Halliburton is rolling its wheels,
counting its cash and raking in billions
from the flowing oil wells
secured by the blood of our young.
The price of oil has risen to an all-time high.
Nearly 4,000 of our finest now lie dead
and thousands more are marked
physically, emotionally, spiritually
for the rest of their lives.

Over 100,000 slain Iraqis have been "liberated"
as a result of our weapons of mass destruction.
Whether we stay or whether we go,
our national will never be able to make right
the multitude of wrongs we have done
in the name of democracy and freedom.
This was not freedom work,
rather the work of unbridled avarice.

We dare not compare our faith
to the faith of Muslims,
for we have unleashed our destructive power
and sanctioned it with the name of Jesus.
Such blasphemy.
And in the houses of God there are precious
few prophets who speak of our collective sin
and our complicity in this aggression.
Our silence condemns us even more.

Where, oh where did we get the idea
that other folks' lives are worth less than ours?
What had the Iraqis done to us?

What in God's name have we done?
And where is our sense of guilt?
We are a nation that knows not the word
repentance.
And so we stand judged by the world,
by the Iraqis and by the Word we hold so dear.

There is death, destruction and chaos
in the land we came to "liberate."
We have unleashed our weapons of death
in a most impressive fashion
and lost our souls in the process.
The vestiges of our campaign of terror
can be seen in the graves
that mark the Iraqi landscape.
The bodies of the young and the old
are testimony to our cruelty,
to our love of war.

FEELING A DRAFT

Someone must have left a window open
for I feel a slight draft coming on.
War has become our national pastime,
but we're running out of soldiers
to take care of all the hot spots.
Too many cells of insurgents on the loose.
We smash 'em here and they pop up there.

We've got the biggest and best guns in the world,
but they're just not doing the job.
We're gonna need more soldiers
to hold down our tenuous positions.

It wasn't supposed to be this way.
It was supposed to be a cake walk.
But now after four years we still
can't claim victory against
a very weak nation with no WMDs.

Let's open up the window real wide
and let the draft on in so that
everybody, every young man and
every young woman can feel the breeze.
War is hell, and it's time
for everyone to know the price
of going to battle on a flimsy excuse.
Let's not just leave it to those from the hood
and white kids from Appalachia.
Let's spread our employment and
our love of war to every household.

Maybe then, and only then, we will cease
viewing war as the latest flick out of Hollywood.

HALF-MAST

Fly the flags at half-mast
for the grief that we
have caused to those
who were not our enemies.

Fly the stars and stripes
at half-mast for the loss
of purity of purpose,
for we have unleashed
our might in evil
and needless ways.

Fly the flags at half-mast
for the soldiers who
die on foreign ground,
those whose families
must also bear the burden
of the finance of war.

Fly the flags at half-mast.
Let truth and justice
reign before we raise
the standard again.

ELECTION DAY

Guided by TV preachers
and sanctimonious pundits,
the Christians surged to the polls
to vote for the candidates
who met the "moral" criteria.
Few of those voters stopped
to think about
what "moral" really means.

No more government
give-aways to the poor.
Give-aways now go to the rich.
Cut those taxes
and keep them down,
award the weapons makers
and excise the poor
for everything they are worth.
It's the Christian thing to do.

National Defense is most important.
Raise the funds for weaponry,
contributing to international suicide.
The weapons might as well
be used on the poor people.
Cutting welfare benefits
is a slower death, though.
It kills old people,
young mothers, little ones....

And the noble, richly blessed Christians
fold their hands over a stuffed turkey,
thankful for all they've
been given this Thanksgiving.

Far too many folks
get their ideas from Pat Robertson
(not exactly the Channel of Love).
Robertson's theme:
"America, take care of thyself.
Let the rest of the world rot."

Joshua reduced his army to 300.
America escalates its
military might and claims
"In God We Trust."

A HORRIBLE TALE OF BUDGETS

There once was a man
who was deeply troubled by
the fact that his family
was spending more
than they were earning.
He stayed up late one night
to figure a way to cut down
on expenses and stay
within the family budget.
"I'll cut back on
my children's food by one half.
Next, there must be no visits
to the doctor for the next year.
In addition, there will be no
more new clothes
purchased either," he concluded.
"I've got to think pragmatically,"
he stated forcefully,
"to get in control of our budget."

While he thought about the budget,
it occurred to him that there
was only one weapon in the home,
a double-barreled shotgun.
"What if three or four
heavily-armed robbers
broke into our home?" he wondered.
The thought was alarming,
to say the least.
He then recalled that
his neighbor had just opened
a gun shop business.

"Wouldn't it be a great gesture
of good will to him
and a safeguard to our family
to buy some of his
best weapons?" he reasoned.

As he was preparing to go to bed
early the next morning,
he noticed his little daughter
playing with, of all things,
the shotgun shells.
She looked up at her shocked father
with one of the bullets in her mouth,
clinched tightly between her teeth.

Absurd, you say?
If you think that is bizarre,
you ought to see what's going on
in Washington these days.